Original title:
Plants and Patience

Copyright © 2025 Creative Arts Management OÜ
All rights reserved.

Author: Adeline Fairfax
ISBN HARDBACK: 978-1-80581-849-6
ISBN PAPERBACK: 978-1-80581-376-7
ISBN EBOOK: 978-1-80581-849-6

Nature's Gentle Timekeeper

In the garden, time just sways,
A tomato waits for sunny days.
The carrots play hide and seek,
While the weeds grow strong and peak.

Squirrels steal acorns, what a fuss,
Nature chuckles, 'It's just us!'
The flowers giggle as they bloom,
'We're just trying to find some room!'

The Heart of Harmony

In a patch, the herbs conspire,
A spice parade, a fragrant choir.
Chives joke, 'Don't give me the thyme!'
While basil ad-libs a catchy rhyme.

Sunflowers sway to music bright,
Dancing daily, what a sight!
The peas roll dice, they're feeling bold,
'Let's gamble on some sunshine gold!'

Nurtured by Silence

A snail's pace in the tender grass,
'Hurry, hurry?' Oh, that's a gas!
While daisies gossip 'neath a cloud,
'We're patiently great,' they say out loud.

The roots have secrets in the depths,
Whispering tales as they take their steps.
The wise old oak just shakes his leaves,
'Chill out, folks, it's all in the eaves!'

Echoes of the Earth

In the soil, laughter's buried deep,
While mosses plot, and shadows creep.
'Where's that worm who borrowed my shades?'
The sprout complains, as sunlight fades.

The wind tells jokes, the branches sway,
As petals giggle, come what may.
'Let's throw a party, we're so spry!'
Let's dance together, just you and I!

Evergreen Endurance

In the garden, a pot stands tall,
With a stubborn cactus, defying it all.
Water me, it shouts, with a tiny grin,
While I laugh, hoping not to drown it in.

Petals of Perseverance

A sunflower dreams to touch the sky,
But gets distracted by bees buzzing by.
'Why wait for sunlight when snacks are near?'
Petals twist in laughter, full of cheer.

The Garden of Tomorrow

In the soil, seeds whisper their plans,
While ants march around like little fans.
'Big dreams!' they chant, 'Can we grow tall?'
But a snail meanders, saying, 'Not at all.'

Quiet Tendrils

Vines stretch out with a curious gaze,
Entangling the garden in a playful maze.
'Who needs a fence?' they giggle and weave,
While the flowers shake their heads, 'Just believe!'

Unraveling in Time

In the garden of growth, things are slow,
Each sprout a secret, waiting to show.
Patience is key, or so they say,
While I munch on snacks, in the sun I lay.

I water with glee, a comedic routine,
Hoping for flowers, but it's mostly green.
My weeds are all winners, they grow with pride,
While my daisies just sit there, they won't abide.

The Maturity of Buds

Little buds giggle, they're shy and sweet,
But wait for the sun, and they'll take the seat.
They plot and they plan, under skies so blue,
While I anxiously wonder what they're up to.

Watching them grow is quite like a show,
They bend to the winds, putting on a flow.
I shout, "Come on, bloom! Don't be such a tease!"
They snicker at me, all the way in the breeze.

Still Waters, Deep Roots

The pond's all quiet, but don't be misled,
Fish gather 'round, whispering dread.
"Will they catch us soon?" they toss and they turn,
While water lilies laugh, "Wait your turn!"

Roots buried deep, like secrets in sleep,
Snails move in stealth, but wishes are cheap.
They're plotting their next great escape from the mud,
Betting on who'll be the first to face the flood.

Nature's Calendar

Seasons roll by like a comic skit,
I mark the days and then call it a hit.
"Today is the day!" I declare with delight,
Only to find it's a Thursday, not bright.

Each leaf takes its time, like the joker in play,
Some stand tall, while the others may sway.
Yet here I am, with a grin across my face,
Waiting for fruit in this patience race.

Tending to Tomorrow

In my garden, weeds do dance,
Spreading chaos with each prance.
I talk to them, they think I'm mad,
But hey, they're the best friends I've had!

Sunflowers stretch up to the sky,
They whisper secrets, oh so sly.
While daisies giggle in a row,
I can't help but laugh at their show!

Seeds of Serenity

I planted seeds in pots of clay,
Waiting for them to sprout one day.
Do they hear my gentle cheer?
Or are they just pretending, I fear?

The carrots grow with little care,
As I converse with the air.
"Hey there, sprout, don't be shy!"
They nod and wink, oh my, oh my!

Cultivating Calm

With watering can, I march about,
Turning the soil without a doubt.
I sing to cabbage, they sway along,
Proving they can dance to my song!

Tomatoes blush under the sun,
They're waiting for a juicy pun.
"Don't stress, dear plants, life's a breeze!"
I promise them, while swatting bees!

Nature's Gentle Rhythm

In the garden, time stands still,
As ants come march, fulfilling a thrill.
I join their parade, pot in hand,
We're a goofy, growing band!

Butterflies flutter, making me laugh,
They land on flowers, oh what a gaff!
I shout, "Take a break, enjoy the chill!"
They roll their wings, what a quirky thrill!

Embracing the Unseen

In the garden, I aim to grow,
A pumpkin that's yet to show.
I water and wait with all my might,
But it still looks like a lump of fright.

Each day I peek, feeling like a fool,
Hoping for magic from this patchy pool.
I swear I saw a sprout today,
But it turned out to be a cat at play.

Patience in the Meadow

In the meadow, flowers wear a frown,
While I'm busy digging up the ground.
They say I should wait, let them bloom slow,
But I'm just hungry for a garden show.

The daisies wink, the grass is tall,
I watch them dance, they seem to stall.
I tell them jokes to help them grow,
But they just chuckle, oh what a show!

The Echo of Roots

Down below, a root sings low,
"I'm deep in the dirt, don't you know?"
While up above, a flower snores,
Dreaming of bugs and open doors.

They boast of growth, I just chuckle,
Waiting for spring while they all snuggle.
I tap my feet and hum a tune,
Will anyone wake up before noon?

Anchored in the Earth

I planted my dreams in a muddy stew,
Mixed them well with a shovel or two.
The weeds just giggle as they spread out wide,
While I sip cold tea and enjoy the ride.

Patience, they shout, it's part of the game,
But I think these roots feel a bit lame.
Each day I water and wiggle my toes,
Hoping for blooms, but here comes more hose!

Tendrils of Time

In the garden, wait and see,
Leaves are stretching endlessly.
Seeds are nudging, taking bets,
On how long before the sweats.

Gnomes are laughing, what a sight,
While the daisies chuckle bright.
But where's the hurry? Oh, my friend,
The sun will rise, this won't end.

Digging holes like t-rexes,
To plant a tree that loves to flex.
It twirls around, it shares its tea,
With worms who dance so happily.

So here we stand, with tools in hand,
Awaiting roots to bless this land.
Time moves slow, like snails on bikes,
Let joy grow up, as nature strikes.

The Thriving Pause

A tiny sprout, not in a rush,
Just chilling out, no fight or fuss.
While we fret about the clock,
It giggles slow, on solid rock.

Rain is pouring like a joke,
The peas look up, and then they poke.
"Hey, the sun was here before,
But now it seems it's gone for a tour!"

Moles are plotting underground,
With visions of snacks they have found.
They're quietly waiting for the sun,
To light up the fun, oh, what a run!

So let it grow, and just enjoy,
This wonderland of green, oh boy!
With every stretch and twist it makes,
In the lively dance, who needs mistakes?

Embracing the Long Game

In a garden bed, I lay my bets,
Soil's my poker face, no regrets.
Worms are my dealers, slow but sly,
Waiting for blooms, oh me, oh my!

I sprinkle water like magic dust,
Hoping for petals, it's a must.
But weeds are laughing, they stole the show,
Guess I'll just drink coffee and go slow!

Veins of Verdancy

Green thumbs are nice, they say with cheer,
But I've got brown, much to my fear.
Cacti won't die, they just roll their eyes,
While daisies plot my comedic demise.

Gardening shows say, 'Add a little flair,'
But my herbs are in hiding, they don't want to share.
I whisper sweet nothings, they just sigh,
"Water us more, or say goodbye!"

Serenity in Sowing

I sprinkle seeds in a dance of glee,
Imagining hugs from a grand old tree.
But squirrels are the thieves of my good intent,
Stealing my visions, it's quite the torment!

With every sprinkle, I do a little jig,
My plants stare back, "You're such a big fig!"
Their roots are tangled, laughing so loud,
At my hopeful smiles, and dreams unbowed!

Echoes of Evergreen

I chat with my ferns, call them my friends,
They nod with leaves, but rarely pretend.
"Grow fast!" I shout, they take their sweet time,
While I'm here pacing, losing my rhyme.

In the jungle of pots, who's in control?
My succulents smirk, they're on a slow stroll.
But one day I'll trip on this green-thumbed fate,
And find my garden is one hell of a state!

The Strength of Softness

Tiny seeds in soil, they peek,
Sunshine tickles, makes them sleek.
They stretch and yawn, greet the day,
Saying, "We'll grow our funny way!"

Worms waltz around, doing the twist,
Giggles shake leaves, can't resist.
Breezy whispers share their schemes,
"Let's grow tall and steal some beams!"

Raindrops dance like they're on stage,
Every leaf a visage, faux rage.
Roots deep down, a ticklish race,
"Who's got the best underground space?"

Even daisies put on a show,
With petals flaunting in a row.
"We're not just flowers, oh so grand,
We're clowns in this garden band!"

Pause and Prevail

A little sprout with dreams so bright,
Asks a rock, "Can I take flight?"
The rock just chuckles, says, "Oh dear,
You've got time; don't shed a tear!"

A sunflower stares at the sky,
"Do I blossom or just sigh?"
"You might just be a king one day,
But first enjoy this sunny play!"

Ants parade in tiny lines,
Carrying crumbs; how it shines!
"Slow down, friends, see the bloom,
Life's a dance, not just a room!"

And in the end, with a twist of fate,
The sprout grows strong—it's never late.
With a wink at the stone, it can't resist,
"I told you, patience has its gist!"

Whispering Vines

Vines that giggle as they climb,
Whisper secrets, full of rhyme.
"Hold on tight, don't let go fast,
Life's a slow and silly blast!"

Berries chuckle in the sun,
"Why rush when we can have some fun?"
"Grow wild and free, that's our aim,
Let each twist be part of the game!"

The willow sways, with a grin so wide,
"Join the dance, let's take a ride!"
Breeze abounds, they laugh and sigh,
"We'll conquer skies, just you and I!"

Time unfolds in nature's grace,
Each leaf a joke, a silly face.
With patience wrapped in laughter's thread,
Whispering vines don't fill with dread!

Nature's Timeless Embrace

Roots hold firm, while branches sway,
Nature chuckles at the play.
"Hello there sun, ready to beam?
Let's make this a hilarious dream!"

A squirrel scurries with acorn in tow,
"What's the rush? It's all in the flow!"
"I'll hide this treasure, then tease and prank,
Just wait, you'll see, I have the rank!"

Clouds drift by, wearing silly hats,
"Look at us float, aren't we bats?"
Each raindrop sings a funny tune,
While flowers dance beneath the moon.

Yet beneath it all, life's goofy cheer,
With every sprout and every year,
Time's slow laughter grows bright and loud,
In nature's arms, we're all so proud!

A Tapestry of Stillness

In the garden, weeds are bold,
They dance around, a sight to behold.
Meanwhile, seeds sit in their bed,
Dreaming of how they'll soon be fed.

The sun shines bright, a blazing foe,
While roots do nothing, just take it slow.
Patience is a flower's way,
As bugs munch leaves and make them sway.

A gnome stands guard, with crooked grin,
Wondering when the fun begins.
His hat is worn, his eyes are keen,
He waits for greens in saturated sheen.

Soon, blossoms burst with colors grand,
But the gnome just yawns, takes a stand.
He mutters, "Is there no quick fix?
I could have used a T-Rex mix?"

Verdant Vows

Roots whispered secrets underground,
While branches swayed, no urgency found.
A snail slides by, its pace a jest,
Claiming, "I'm just on a leisurely quest!"

Sunflowers tall, they scratch their heads,
Wondering what path the bumblebee treads.
The daisies giggle, "We're fashionably late,
But life's too short for a race or a fate!"

A vine creeps slowly, giving a wink,
As clovers chat in a synchronous blink.
"I swear," they say, "tonight we will bloom,
If only someone clears the room!"

The wise old tree, with a sigh so deep,
Laughs softly: "Let's not lose sleep.
Growth takes time, just like fine cheese,
Or waiting on a pest to sneeze!"

Sun-Kissed Waiting

In this bright patch, the sun plays tricks,
While leafy greens cling like sticky licks.
Frogs croak songs, absurd and loud,
Their chorus forms a patient crowd.

A ladybug dines on tender leaves,
Sipping dew like she's at a feast.
The daisies play their waiting game,
While grass blades poke and try to claim.

Time's a trickster with funny rules,
The garden knows it's not for fools.
A hermit crab shows up for a tour,
Advises, "Just chill, be slow, for sure!"

As night falls down, the stars take flight,
The flowers close, snuggled tight.
In the morning, they will awake,
With bright dreams of the day's next stake!

The Promise Underfoot

Down below, a party brews,
Where worms and soil swap their news.
A chipmunk pops, acts like a host,
Saying, "Roots are waiting for a robust toast!"

The daisies gossip about the rain,
While rabbits claim they'll never complain.
"Hey, look at us!" they beam and say,
"We enjoy the art of vague ballet!"

A mushroom winks, but holds its ground,
Pledging to pop up without making a sound.
Patience is their fun little game,
As bugs take bets on who's to blame.

Underfoot, the world spins fun,
With seeds and beats that never run.
So let's just relish in this dirt,
And laugh at how we often flirt!

Green Thumb Wisdom

In the garden, I do cheer,
Watering weeds, oh what a fear!
With every sprout, a giggle groans,
I'm just here chatting with garden gnomes.

Wait, is that a leaf or just some fluff?
I'm not a medic, but this is tough!
I talk to daisies, they just stare,
Guess they think I'm quite the square!

Sunflowers stretch, but I just sigh,
While I try my best to comply.
They say a garden needs some time,
I'll just sip my drink, and rhyme.

Soon they'll bloom, or so they claim,
Every day feels just the same.
But who needs blooms when I've got cheer?
At least my garden gives me beer!

Whispers of Growth

I planted seeds, what did I do?
Germs must be laughing at my view.
I sprinkle hope like it's confetti,
But it seems my patience is quite unsteady.

Each day I peek, it's just bare earth,
Where's my basil? I need its worth!
The carrots mock, they're taking their time,
Perhaps I should plant them in a nursery rhyme.

I fertilize and then drink tea,
My plan is brilliant! You'll see, you'll see!
But earthworms wriggle, they get the prize,
They laugh at my efforts and my silly cries.

When they eventually sprout up, I'll cheer,
For now, I'll stroll to the fridge for a beer.
My green thumb needs a little rest,
Next season, I'll surely be the best!

The Dance of Seasons

Winter's chill, I plant in the snow,
The seeds just laugh, they don't want to grow.
Come spring, I'm back, with shovel and scoff,
But the plants just yawn, and then fall off.

A summer sun that's hot as can be,
But my herbs just frown, 'Oh, let us be!'
I swear I heard my tomatoes pout,
As they silently plotted to jump right out.

Then autumn comes, what a sight to see,
Leaves a-dancing, they'd rather be free.
I've grown a jungle that's mostly weeds,
While critters feast on my stubborn seeds.

Yet in this mess, I still find a grin,
For every failure, a cheeky win.
Who knew green dreams could be such a hoot?
I'll keep on planting; it's all quite cute!

Unseen Progress

I check my plants; they're just standing still,
I swear I watered with just the right skill.
'Grow faster!' I cry, in sheer disbelief,
But they're likely plotting behind my belief.

I talk to the mud, it's what friends do,
But it whispers back, 'We're not ready for you!'
With each passing day, my patience on breath,
Do I entice them with dirt and a wreath?

One lonely sprout, it waves with a grin,
"Just wait for the party—we'll soon begin!"
Yet all the while, the weeds throw a rave,
I pull them out gently, misbehaving knaves.

But the sun is shining, and hope finds a way,
With warmth in my heart, I'll dance 'til the day.
For unseen growth is the trick of the game,
Next spring, I'll own this gardening fame!

Roots that Bide

Deep below, they wiggle and giggle,
Holding on tight, without a single squibble.
Staying calm, through storm and sun,
Roots just chill, while above, we run.

With all that waiting, they've mastered the game,
Watching folks hustle, but feel no shame.
They'll grow with a chuckle, often unseen,
Making sure they're living the root-iful dream.

Serenity in Soil

In the dirt, where whispers are heard,
The earthworms chuckle, it's truly absurd!
A little seed giggles, 'I'm not in a race!'
Settling down with a smiling face.

Not bothered by weeds or occasional rain,
They've got their zen, all wrapped in terrain.
With a stretch and a yawn, they're in their own groove,
Dancing in silence—a plant-napping move.

The Gentle Gift of Growth

Each morning, a sprout waves hello,
With a gentle yawn, it puts on a show.
No need for a rush, it simply unfolds,
While sipping on sunshine, content and bold.

The petals laugh softly, a colorful jest,
Saying, "Slow your roll, we'll grow with zest!"
They bloom with amusement, no stress in sight,
Enjoying their time, reaching for light.

Journey of the Seed

A tiny seed, with dreams and plans,
Rolls through dirt, with small little fans.
'Watch me sprout!' it shouts with glee,
As ants march by, ordering tea.

Patience, my friend, it knows no haste,
For greatness blooms, but it takes some taste.
A slow dance of fate, with nature's own tune,
Daring to grow, beneath the bright moon.

Flourishing Under Foot

In a pot on the sill, a cactus stands tall,
Eager for sunlight, yet so very small.
It looks like a king, but needs just a sip,
Oh, how it grumbles when I take a trip.

My basil's a diva, it demands some flair,
With whispers of pesto, it fills the air.
Yet, water it once, and it throws a fit,
Next thing I know, it's throwing a witt!

The Weaving of Green

A fern in the corner, it's waving hello,
Trying to sprout where the breezes do blow.
It fluffs up its fronds, quite the delicate sweep,
Yet wonders at night why I'm still counting sheep.

The ivy clings tight, like a toddler's hold,
Asking for sunshine, bathing in gold.
Tangled and twisted, it plays tag with the wall,
A green little rascal, it's having a ball.

Silent Symphonies of Soil

In a pot full of dirt, a radish does sigh,
Dreaming of salad, reaching for the sky.
With each passing day, it giggles and grunts,
"I'm not just a veggie, I'm full of fun hunts!"

The worms down below have their own jolly tune,
Dancing to earthbeats, they're quite the monsoon.
They dig tunnels of laughter, squirming with glee,
Making the moles think they're in a spree.

The Cadence of Greenery

A clumsy old palm, it sways and it swerves,
Saying it's graceful, but losing its curves.
Each leaf tells a joke, waving wildly about,
"Who knew being green could lead to a pout?"

And in a bright corner, my poor spider plant,
It's growing more babies than I ever grant.
Hanging on threads, like a circus on pause,
Flipping me off with its leafy "What's cause?"

From Seedling to Serenity

A tiny seed just found its way,
Eager to sprout in sunny array.
But wait! A bird chose that same spot,
And now it's a game of beak and plot.

Digging deep, it took its time,
With roots in soil, feeling sublime.
A worm came by, said, "What's the rush?"
"We'll party later, in the hush!"

Leaves stretched wide, a leafy cheer,
"Do you smell sunshine? It's finally here!"
But then a squirrel, oh what a tease,
Decided to play hide and seek with ease.

So now we wait, and laugh a lot,
As our garden dances in sunlight hot.
We're sprouting joy, and what's the fuss?
Who knew, growth could come with such a plus?

Cultivating Calm

With watering can in hand, I vow,
Today I'll tend my leafy cow.
She wobbles, she shakes, with a giggle or two,
But watering her is no easy zoo!

A dosing of patience, the label said,
I squint at weeds that dance in my head.
One flower whispers, "Chill out dude,"
While another moans, "Where's my food?"

Each day I toil, with humor and glee,
Weeding and chatting, just my plants and me.
And when they bloom, I'll shout a cheer,
"Who knew gardening could bring such beer?"

So here we grow, with laughter in tow,
Taking every misstep like a pro.
Oh, life in the garden is simply a dream,
With giggles galore and sunlight's gleam.

The Art of Waiting

In a pot too small, a seed sits tight,
Dreaming of green in the pale moonlight.
"Is it lunch yet?" the sprout starts to pout,
While wise old dirt says, "Just chill out!"

The sun shifts high, the rain does fall,
He peeks each day, and still feels small.
His roots tickle gently in the soil's bliss,
But someone needs to teach him patience, I guess!

Days mix into weeks, as he learns to sway,
"Should I dance now?" he mused, in dismay.
A neighbor leaf laughed, "Don't rush like me,
We'll have a fiesta, beneath the tree!"

Finally, in bloom, he grinned wide and bright,
"Waiting was fun, look at the light!"
So, growing up can take a while,
But trust me friend, it's worth the trial!

Blossoms in the Breeze

A flower danced in the summer air,
Swaying with joy and a curly hair.
"Hey, look at me!" it shouted aloud,
While whispers of petals formed a crowd.

A bee buzzed close, "Oh, what a show!"
"Watch the wind dip low, then up we go!"
"Let's tease the grass, let's twirl and spin,
Growing up tall is just pure win!"

But suddenly a storm rolled in with a frown,
The petals all ducked, and some tumbled down.
"Not the end!" said a brave little bud,
"We'll bounce back up, just watch us, dud!"

And soon the sun shone, the sky was blue,
With all their laughter, they knew what to do.
They twirled and bounced, full of glee,
As blossoms in the breeze, wild and free!

A Garden of Stillness

In my backyard, weeds throw a dance,
They wiggle and jiggle, not a second chance.
I planted some tomatoes, gave them a chat,
They just sat there, looking so flat.

Each morning I water, with hope in my eyes,
But all I hear back are crickets and sighs.
I sing to my flowers, they look quite aloof,
Clearly, they've settled, beneath the green roof.

The carrots are hiding, the radishes too,
They must be planning a vegetable coup.
I've struck an accord with the snails at night,
They promise to sprout, if I keep them in sight.

So here I am packing my fortune in dirt,
Waiting for magic, or at least spade and shirt.
Maybe next summer, I'll have quite the spread,
For now, my garden's just mostly misread.

Attentive Hearts

I whisper sweet nothings to my little plants,
They roll their green eyes and do little dances.
The sun's shining brightly, but they just don't care,
I'm starting to think, they thrive on my despair.

The other day, my basil looked quite blue,
I asked what was wrong, it said, "You too!"
So here I sit, offering therapy sessions,
But all I get back are minimal expressions.

She said, "Just be still, let nature unfold,
Our secrets are deep, and not bought or sold."
With that, I just laughed, taken by surprise,
A sage in a pot with expansive ideas.

Now we share stories, on the patio wide,
I tend to our chats, with jasmine as guide.
A bond of the weird, with roots intertwined,
Learning together, oh what a find!

Lessons from the Soil

What wisdom lies deep in this earth I tend?
For every tiny sprout, there's time to spend.
I learned from my carrots, they thrive in the dark,
But get too much sunlight, they're just a cold spark.

The radishes rush; they're always in a hurry,
Popping up quick, then they start to worry.
"Where's the excitement?" said one under leaf,
I chuckled and told him, "It's all about belief!"

The daisies grinned as they laughed at their fate,
Growing in places that made folks irate.
With roots wrapped around, they stand proud and small,
Teaching us all, to be sturdy and tall.

So gather your lessons from the soil below,
Where every seed sown is a chance to grow.
And if something wilts, just give it a go,
With patience and giggles, life will start to flow.

The Blossoming Heart

When spring arrives knocking, my heart starts to race,
With petals in bloom, it's a curious chase.
I'll gather my seeds and mix sunshine and glee,
But every time they sprout, they giggle at me.

My daisies insist that they know how to dance,
While hollyhocks plot in a festive romance.
One sunflower whispered to me with a grin,
"Patience, my friend, let the fun begin!"

And though I'm a gardener with dreams oh-so-big,
I find I chuckle, when I step on the sprig.
They flourish in chaos, in laughter and light,
Reminding me gently, it's all quite all right.

So here's to the blooms, with laughter entwined,
In the story of growth, there's joy to be mined.
My heart learns to blossom, in colors and cheer,
With every new sprout, a reminder draws near.

Hope's Hidden Garden

In the corner, a pot sways,
With a stubborn sprout that plays.
It winks at me, all shy and spry,
Claiming it's a tree, oh my!

I water it with a song or two,
Hoping it'll grow nice and true.
But all it does is drink and grin,
I swear it's planning a leafy spin!

The weeds are my true frenemy,
They tease me with their symmetry.
I've tried to uproot each autumn,
Yet they come back, now I'm their dumb-dumb!

But in this mess, I find some cheer,
A garden of giggles, it's clear.
For sprouting joy is worth the fight,
In a pot of dreams, oh what a sight!

Sunlit Paths of Patience

There's a snail on the sidewalk, what a sight,
Slowly moving to its left and right.
I cheer it on with loud, silly cheers,
"Keep it up, buddy! You've got no fears!"

The daisies giggle with their whitish heads,
Poking fun at thorns in their beds.
"Ha! You're prickly, we're soft and sweet,
Come join us for tea, it's quite a treat!"

And here I am, sprawled on the ground,
Watching the bees make a silly sound.
"Hey, Mr. Bumble, lost your way?
Your dance is wild, in broad daylight!"

Oh, the sun shines on all their deeds,
As laughter sprouts from roots and seeds.
In this strange world of giggly green,
I find my joy in the scenes unseen!

Crafting Quietude

In tiny pots, a jungle stirs,
Amidst the chaos, a calm occurs.
I sip my tea, while basil sighs,
"Can't you see? We're wise guys!"

My cactus winks, it's quite the joker,
No water for me, I'm a real poker!
"Who needs drinks? Just bring the light,
With sunshine on my spines, I'll be alright!"

A chive tries to steal the show,
"It's time for puns! Join in the flow."
I giggle loud, my heart's a flutter,
While thyme rolls its eyes, "That's just clutter!"

In this quiet nook of humored dismay,
I find my peace in the playful display.
For in every leaf, a story sings,
Crafting joy from the smallest things!

The Language of Green

The ferns converse in flips and flops,
While I decipher their leafy hops.
A parley of petals, quite absurd,
Their giggles follow every word!

"Oh look! There's a gnome, trying to hide,
Thought he could fool us, what a ride!"
Hydrangeas blush in shades of blue,
"Let's tell him a secret, just me and you!"

The sunflowers nod in tall accord,
"We'll keep it hush, not a single word."
While toadstools giggle from the ground,
In this secret world, laughter's found.

As leaves whisper tales of joy and jest,
I learn a lesson from their playful quest.
In the garden's humor, patience blooms,
In every corner, magic looms!

The Unhurried Journey

In the garden, time don't race,
A snail took up a prime parking space.
He gazes at the flowers with glee,
Dreaming of petals his friends can't see.

A pesky worm trails behind so slow,
He murmurs, "Why rush? The sun's aglow!"
While bees zoom by, swift as a dart,
The chill of patience warms his heart.

With each droplet of dew like a party glass,
The wait makes the blooms even more of a class.
So dance in the breeze, take a seat on the ground,
The best things in life simply come around.

Joking with daisies, he shouts, "Let's chill!"
Grow old by the day, but who's keeping still?
Laughing at time, with roots buried deep,
While others rush in, he's living the leap.

Resilience in Green

A cactus in the corner, prickly and spry,
Says to the fern, "You can't rush to fly!"
The fern giggles softly, dancing in shade,
"I thrive in the slow lane, and I'm never afraid!"

Lettuce tries jogging, but wobbles instead,
While carrots are lounging, just chilling in bed.
"Come join our weekend!" the tomatoes all cheer,
With vines intertwined, there's nothing to fear.

Each seed knows the drill, it's a waiting game,
But the laughs that they share? Now that's the fame!
With roots so determined and dreams set to sprout,
They remind us all: patience is what it's about.

So if you're rushing, just take a seat,
Grab leafy greens and enjoy a sweet treat!
Resilience is funny when viewed through their eyes,
A garden of laughter beneath sunny skies.

A Tapestry of Time

In a patchwork of colors, a daffodil sways,
Stitching together the sunniest rays.
While lilacs debate if they should bloom first,
"Let's take our time!" they happily burst.

The roses complain, "What a slow-moving show!"
But daisies retort, "Just go with the flow!"
Each petal's a story, a giggle, a cheer,
Time sails on by; there's nothing to fear.

Sunflowers tower, their heads in the sky,
While some are just short, who cares? Not I!
They huddle together and tell silly tales,
"How wide is the world?!» Each rant never pales.

A tapestry woven, with patience as thread,
Each stitch is a joke that they love to spread.
As seasons unwind, watch laughter unfurl,
In the garden of time, what a whimsical world!

The Heart of the Harvest

In the veggie patch, they take it real slow,
With peas in a pod, they put on a show!
They brag about growth, yet they're hardly tall,
"Big dreams take time, we're living it all!"

The pumpkins are plotting a world-fair race,
While radishes giggle, "Not in my case!"
They whisper and chuckle at how time will tell,
"Ain't rushing this harvest; we're doing it well!"

Each fruit has its own schedule, it's clear,
A banana can't rush; it's in for a year!
But every wait's worth it, they know it's no doubt,
The punchline's the juiciest, the taste that's about.

So raise your glass high for the fruits of the field,
Where patience and humor are perfectly healed.
In the heart of each gathering, laughter does thrive,
With a joke in the soil, best times come alive!

The Dance of the Unseen

Underneath the soil they sway,
Tiny dancers in their ballet.
Roots in slippers, mud on their toes,
Who knew dirt could have fancy shows?

Worms in tuxedos, all dressed in grime,
Conducting a symphony, oh, what a crime!
They twirl and spin, just out of sight,
Making their moves in the dead of night.

Sunshine tickles, rain sings along,
In this hush, they hum their song.
Though we can't see, they'll never yield,
The silent circus, nature's field.

So next time you dig, don't scoff or pout,
There's a party down there, without a doubt!
With laughs and giggles beneath our feet,
Nature's jesters, who never retreat.

Tender Mutations

In the garden, something's a-shift,
Leaves are laughing, giving us a gift.
A cactus dressed up in a frilly gown,
Says, "Come for tea, but do sit down!"

Tomatoes chuckle, ripe and round,
Whispering secrets from underground.
Zucchini wearing a party hat,
Invites the peas to dance with a cat!

Carrots gossip about their roots,
Swapping stories of daring shoots.
While the radishes, in tutus, twirl,
In this wild world, laughter does swirl.

Oh, the mischief that nature conspires,
With roots and leaves, never tires.
In the soil, joy blooms bright and bold,
With every sprout, a tale unfolds!

Roots of Resilience

Beneath the surface, a tale unfolds,
Of plants so brave, and stories told.
With roots that wiggle and twist with pride,
They hold each other, a strong divide.

"Can we stretch further?" one leaf did muse,
"We could reach the sky, what have we to lose?"
The others giggled, "A bit of rain,
Might just send us soaring again!"

Through storms and drought, they stand so tall,
With nature's laughter they conquer all.
"Let's take a selfie," said a sprightly vine,
"Grinning with roots, we're doing just fine!"

So raise a glass to our leafy friends,
And celebrate how resilience bends.
In their green hearts, a humorous spark,
Life and laughter bloom in the dark.

Blooming in Silence

In the quiet hours, blooms start to play,
Fluffy petals pirouette in the sway.
No fanfare needed, just a gentle breeze,
A daisy giggles, "I do it with ease!"

Lilies whisper, "What color shall we be?"
An orange one chortles, "I'll just be me!"
With pigments splashing in soft sunlight,
Amidst all laughter, they're quite a sight!

"Don't forget the bees!" a sunflower shouts,
They buzz in, wearing fluffy green spouts.
"Just pollinate gently, don't make a fuss,
With all of this blooming, we're on the bus!"

So here in the calm, where colors ignite,
Nature's humor sparkles in the light.
And if you listen, 'neath blossoms' delight,
A silent chuckle will take off in flight.

Evergreen Endurance

In a pot sits a sprout, looking quite small,
Waiting for sunlight, in hopes it won't fall.
It dreams of the day when it'll grow tall,
But right now it's just a green little ball.

With care and some water, it stretches its limbs,
Trying hard daily, but looks like a whim.
"Oh, I can't wait!" it chirps with a grin,
"Just give me a chance, I'll soon wear a trim!"

Each tumble of dirt feels like a big jump,
"Oh look at me, I'm a big, strong lump!"
But when the cat saunters, it gives quite a yelp,
And curls back up like a frightened little kelp.

Yet with every small leaf that pops out of fright,
It cheers for each inch—a true display of might!
"Oh, come on, sunshine, just give me your light,
I promise to grow—you'll see, what a sight!"

Blooms in the Breeze

Little buds hover, they sway with a dance,
Wishing for pollen, a sweet, flowery chance.
While giggling and twisting, they twirl and prance,
"Don't be shy, tiny bee, join in our romance!"

A dandelion beams, all parts of a plan,
"Watch me transform—I'll be more than a fan!
From a weed to a wish, I'll get my own can,
Just wait and see, I'm the best in the land!"

The lilies keep gossiping, gaily they tease,
"Have you heard what she said, just blowing in the breeze?
I mean, really, come on, where's her big leaves?
She's barely a bud, but thinks she's a tease!"

Yet smiles abound in this garden of glee,
Each trying their fate with no hurry to flee.
In hues where they bicker, it's clear as can be,
The best kind of waiting is totally free!

A Season's Patience

Spring woke up chirping, the flowers all yawn,
While winter still whispers, "You're early, hold on!"
Yet sprouts in the soil pretend they're all gone,
As they nap in the gloom, from dusk until dawn.

"Is it time?" one shoots, peeking out for a glance,
"Will I be in bloom, or should I take a chance?"
But no one replies, just a slow, lazy dance,
As frost gives a snicker, "You're part of my trance!"

Up pops a tulip, so bold and so bright,
"It's my time to shine! You all get it right?"
But laughter erupts from the buds hidden tight,
"Oh please, tiny friend, you're just starting tonight!"

With seasons of laughter, these green friends unfold,
In times often silly, patience strikes gold.
"For we'll bloom together, just watch as we mold,
A garden of chuckles, a sight to behold!"

The Subtle Unfolding

A tiny green shoot gives a cautious stretch,
"Am I ready to grow? I think I'm a wretch!"
As neighbors around whisper, "Here, give us a sketch,
We'll cheer for your sprout, as we play our fetch!"

The roots take a trip, unaware of their fate,
"Is this soil too rich? Or am I late?"
While ants pass by, with food on their plate,
"This plant is a riot! Can't wait for a mate!"

A leaf finally pops, like a kid at a show,
"Look, Mom, I'm a leaf! I'm starting to grow!"
But laughter erupts, for it steals the slow flow,
"I'm tired of waiting; onward I go!"

Yet with every twist, the sunlight will cheer,
"Just take your own time; there's nothing to fear.
In this game of growth, you're the star, my dear,
Just don't get too big, you might lose your sphere!"

Roots of Resilience

In a pot sat a cactus, quite quiet and shy,
With spines like a hedgehog, it aimed for the sky.
Friends called it prickly, but with charm it would sway,
"I'm just growing slowly, enjoy the sun's ray!"

A sprout in the corner just wiggled with glee,
"Look how tall I am! Can't you see me?"
But the others just chuckled, with roots that run deep,
"You'll catch up one day; for now, take a leap!"

An old fern told a tale of patience in leaves,
"I waited for ages, but now I'm a breeze!"
The others all laughed, as they reached for some light,
"You'll grow green and proud while we bask in delight!"

So they danced all around with their quirks and their quirks,
In a garden of giggles and funny little quirks.
Every inch of the soil held dreams to ignite,
The roots would unite in the warm afternoon light!

Whispering Vines

A vine whispered secrets to a tall, lumbering tree,
"Why don't you run faster? Come join me with glee!"
The tree let out a chuckle, swaying in the breeze,
"I'm rooted down solid; you're just a tease!"

They played peek-a-boo with the sun's golden rays,
The vine coiled and twisted in high acrobatic ways.
Suddenly it tripped, and with a tumble it fell,
"Who knew being flashy could lead to such hell!"

The tree shook its branches, dusted off the vine,
"Come back up, dear friend, everything's fine!"
"But I wanted to dazzle, climb high to the moon,
Your sturdy old trunk doesn't dance or croon!"

With laughter they both swayed in the soft summer air,
Offering shades, roots, and a love that they share.
Together they learned, through their fun little rifts,
That patience is magic wrapped up in slow shifts!

The Silent Growth

In stillness they grow, the quiet little sprouts,
While humans rush by with their loud, hurried shouts.
"Hurry up!" they say, as they race along fast,
But the little ones giggle, knowing time's a blast!

A shy little bulb boasted, "I'll bloom one fine day!"
The others just nodded, "We'll watch on the way!"
In the dark, it blinked slowly, counting each star,
"I'll show them all soon, just wait - not too far!"

Carrots chuckled deeply beneath layers of dirt,
"Take your time friends, no need for the hurt!"
They watched as a snail made a break for the sun,
"Just a step at a time makes it all a bit fun!"

And days turned to weeks; they giggled with glee,
As petals unfurled and they danced in the breeze.
Who knew that such growth could transform just a patch,
In a garden of patience, they found the best match!

Beneath the Surface

Beneath the dark soil, a party took place,
With all sorts of roots having fun in their space.
"Let's stretch a bit farther!" called out one just shy,
"I cannot grow up if I can't reach the sky!"

A bulb with a giggle said, "Wait for a beat,
Let's savor the moment, make this grand retreat!"
While worms wiggled close, doing a jolly old dance,
The roots joined in laughter, given the chance!

"Dig deeper, dig deeper!" a sprout gave a shout,
But some roots were just cozy, they didn't want out.
"Why rush to the surface? The view will not fade,
We can be quite content in the shade that we made!"

And so they all settled, in laughter they grew,
Finding joy in the waiting—their patience, like glue.
In the dark they all thrived, in a party sublime,
"There's magic in quiet; it's simply our time!"

The Pursuit of Growth

In a pot, a sprout does dream,
But it's stuck, it's quite the theme.
Water me now, oh please don't wait,
Or I might just grow a little late!

Sunshine's peeking, what's the deal?
It's time to stretch, to spin the wheel!
Yet here I am, just feeling shy,
Waiting for my moment to fly!

A worm stares up, says, "What's the fuss?"
I tell him, "Growth's a slow bus!"
He chuckles back, with a wiggle and grin,
Reminding me, it's fun to begin!

So let me bask in this slow parade,
While friends around me make the grade.
With roots that dance underground a tad,
I'll bloom one day; it can't be bad!

Waiting for the Rain

The sky is blue, but I'm a bit dry,
"Oh rain!" I shout, with a hopeful sigh.
My leaves are wilting, feeling quite glum,
But look at the squirrel—he's having fun!

He's dancing 'round in the morning light,
While I just hope for a drop tonight.
"Don't rush it," he says, with a cheeky wink,
"Enjoy the sunshine, and give it a think!"

I'd love to stretch, but I'm stuck in place,
Like a tortoise in an endless race.
The clouds look thick, but they need some time,
So I'll just relax and sip on some mime!

And when the rain comes, oh what a thrill!
I'll drink it up, I'll get my fill.
So here I'll wait, with a groan and a grin,
For that sweet, sweet storm to let the fun begin!

Nature's Unhurried Artistry

In gardens wide, they slowly twirl,
The flowers scheme, the petals curl.
A daisy yawns, "What's the rush?"
While wildflowers giggle—a little hush!

The trees stand tall, in robes of green,
Awaiting the breeze, so calm and serene.
"Why hurry up?" the daisies shout,
"We'll bloom in time—there's never a doubt!"

A bumblebee buzzes with a lazy tune,
Waltzing around like it owns the afternoon.
It stops to choose, "I'll eat this one, too!"
Nature's buffet is endless and true!

So join the parade, let's take a stroll,
Through fields of laughter—it's good for the soul.
With every step, we'll laugh and sigh,
For beauty takes time, and we just can't fly!

Gentle Seasons, Gentle Souls

Spring grumbles, with a sleepy start,
While winter's chill still lingers in heart.
"Refill my cup!" says the old oak tree,
"You'd think it's April, but where's my glee?"

The birds are late, they took a wrong train,
They land with a thud, but they'll entertain!
"Sorry we're tardy!" they chirp in delight,
"Just had to stop for a quick coffee bite!"

Summer arrives, and the daisies yawn,
"Let's lounge around till the break of dawn!"
While cheeky sparrows make quite the fuss,
And soak in the sun—what's all the rush?

As autumn creeps in, it whispers low,
"Change takes its time, don't tell me to go!"
So we sway in the breeze, with roots so deep,
These gentle souls dance—ah, what a leap!

Seasons of Stillness

In spring, the seeds are full of glee,
They wiggle and dance as if they're free.
But weeks go by with nary a sprout,
They joke, 'Maybe we're just very stout!'

Summer sun brings a sticky haze,
We water and fuss in a grateful daze.
Yet the plants just laugh, all green and bold,
'We're taking our time, if truth be told!'

Autumn whispers, 'Don't rush the show,'
As leaves drop down in a drowsy flow.
The garden sings, with a chuckle and cheer,
'We'll bloom when we want, please save your fear!'

Winter wraps up the silent plot,
The frozen ground's a cozy spot.
With frost and snow, they twirl and spin,
'Who said this rest isn't a win?'

Tending to Time

Watering cans and silly hats,
Digging holes for very fat rats.
With every droplet, they lounge and sigh,
'We're waiting for dinner, don't even try!'

The clock ticks loud, but they won't budge,
Roots like to nap; oh, don't you judge!
With every weed pulled, they snicker and jest,
'Can't you see? This is our quest!'

A gardener's patience is tried and tested,
While greens on the ground remain unvested.
They chuckle together, roots intertwined,
'Slow and steady? Oh, how refined!'

As moonlight glows on the dormant scene,
They dream of the things they might have been.
In the lull, they grin, content and sly,
'Why rush the fun? We're in no hurry, bye!'

Nature's Quiet Wisdom

In every garden, wisdom flows,
With leafy giggles from rows to rows.
They say, 'Who needs speed while we can tease?
Growing takes time—let's take it with ease!'

Sunshine teases with rays of gold,
But plants have secrets, a tale to be told.
'Put down those shears; we'll sprout when we game,
We're not racing—much too mundane!'

The insects buzz with sage wisdom clear,
'Growth is an art, my dear, never fear!'
They sip on dew and share bloomin' thoughts,
'What's the rush? Life's more fun when you plot!'

Seasons drift by, but they just munch,
On quiet moments with laughter to crunch.
With joy in the soil, they snicker and blend,
'Who said we need to follow the trend?'

The Slow Unfurling

A sprout peeks out with a sleepy grin,
'Today's the day! Or maybe next win?'
With sun above, they ponder their fate,
'Why not lounge a bit more—don't tempt your mate!'

As colors emerge, they giggle and bounce,
'Our gorgeous greens will make hearts flounce!'
Why hurry this masterpiece in progress?
A garden's a show, not a race to impress!

They toss a few petals in frolicking glee,
'It's art in the making—look and you'll see!'
The buds shake their heads, content with the wait,
'We'll flower in style, just don't set a date!'

So let's not fuss; let the soft wind sing,
For the best things in life are worth waiting.
In the patch of mirth, they find their sweet role,
With nature's own humor woven in soul.

In the Shadow of Leaves

In a pot where growth is slow,
A sprout thinks it's a superstar show.
With sunbathing leaves, it strikes a pose,
But the neighbor's weeds just laugh in rows.

Watering can's a trusty friend,
But too much splash can cause a trend.
The neighbor's cat comes for a drink,
And suddenly, all plants start to shrink.

Chasing shadows on the ground,
A dance of sunlight all around.
The wind joins in with a silly flair,
As petals swirl through garden air.

So here we wait, with bated breath,
For blossoms, blooms, and leafy heft.
We'll cheer them on with every chance,
And hope tomorrow brings the dance!

Flourish in Fidelity

In a tiny pot, a cactus sits,
With spikes that boast of tiny hits.
Its neighbor's jealous; tried to climb,
But fell right off and landed in grime.

Oh, the fern next door loves to spout,
"I'm the best, there is no doubt!"
But every time it takes a leap,
It flops and falls, a funny heap.

The roses giggle in a row,
While daisies put on quite a show.
"Why bother growing high and grand?
Let's lounge instead! That's just our brand!"

In this garden, nothing's steep,
We wait for roots, and don't lose sleep.
With laughter echoing through the year,
What fun it is to grow right here!

Echoes of the Earth

In the patch of dirt, a worm does wave,
"Move aside, I'm here to pave!"
But with every wiggle, it appears,
The flowers giggle, covering their ears.

"Oh look who's shining!" shouts the sun,
As daisies bloom, their day's begun.
Yet when the clouds come rolling in,
They all just sulk, it's quite the din!

A potato dreams of being chic,
"Where's my crown? I'm unique, not meek!"
Yet hidden deep beneath the earth,
It laughs along, embracing worth.

So let's unite in soil and cheer,
For all the giggles that we share here.
With roots that hold and blooms that sway,
Life is jest, come what may!

Transformative Tranquility

A basil leaf dreams of spaghetti,
While thyme rolls in, looking quite jetty.
"If I get spritzed with some fine wine,
The chef will surely say I'm divine!"

In a corner, mint is on a spree,
Sipping water, thinking it's tea.
While all the herbs chase after trends,
The beans just lounge, it's how it ends.

The petals fashion tiny hats,
For squirrels that tease and look like brats.
"Oh what a world, so full of bloom,
Who knew dirt could feel like a room?"

So here we stay, a wild bunch,
Making the most of our garden lunch.
With laughter growing, side by side,
In living soil, we take our ride!